Weather Watchers

Rain

Cassie Mayer

Heinemann
LIBRARY

www.heinemann.co.uk/library
Visit our website to find out more information about **Heinemann Library** books.

To order:
☎ Phone 44 (0) 1865 888066
▤ Send a fax to 44 (0) 1865 314091
▢ Visit the Heinemann Bookshop at www.heinemann.co.uk/library to browse our
catalogue and order online.

First published in Great Britain by Heinemann Library,
Halley Court, Jordan Hill, Oxford OX2 8EJ, part of
Harcourt Education. Heinemann is a registered trademark
of Harcourt Education Ltd.

Editorial: Tracey Crawford, Cassie Mayer, Dan Nunn,
and Sarah Chappelow
Design: Jo Hinton-Malivoire
Picture Research: Tracy Cummins, Tracey Engel,
and Ruth Blair
Production: Duncan Gilbert

Originated by Chroma Graphics (Overseas) Pte. Ltd
Printed and bound in China by South China
Printing Company

10 digit ISBN 0 431 18256 6
13 digit ISBN 978 0 431 18256 8

11 10 09
10 9 8 7 6 5 4 3 2

British Library Cataloguing in Publication Data
Mayer, Cassie
  Rain. - (Weather watchers)
  1.Rain and rainfall - Juvenile literature
  I.Title
  551.5'77
A full catalogue record for this book is available from the
British Library.

Acknowledgements
The publishers would like to thank the following for
permission to reproduce photographs: Corbis pp. **4**
(cloud; sunshine, G. Schuster/zefa), **5** (Anthony Redpath),
14 (Royalty Free), **15** (Bruce Peebles), **18** (ARKO
DATTA/Reuters), **21** (Simon Marcus); Getty Images pp. **4**
(lightning; snow, Marc Wilson Photography), **6** (George
Grall), **16** (Jeremy Woodhouse), **17** (altrendo nature), **19**
(David Woodfall), **20** (Steve Satushek), **23** (cracked clay,
altrendo nature; flood, David Woodfall).

Cover photograph reproduced with permission of Corbis
(Anthony Redpath). Back cover photograph reproduced
with permission of Corbis (ARKO DATTA/Reuters).

Every effort has been made to contact copyright holders
of any material reproduced in this book. Any omissions
will be rectified in subsequent printings if notice is given
to the publishers.

Contents

What is weather? 4

What is rain? 6

Types of rain 14

How does rain help us? 20

What to wear in the rain 22

Picture glossary 23

Index 24

What is weather?

 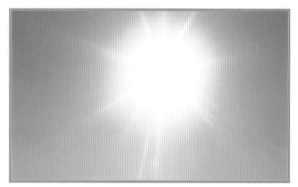

There are many types of weather.
Weather changes all the time.

Rain is a type of weather.

What is rain?

Rain is water that falls from clouds.

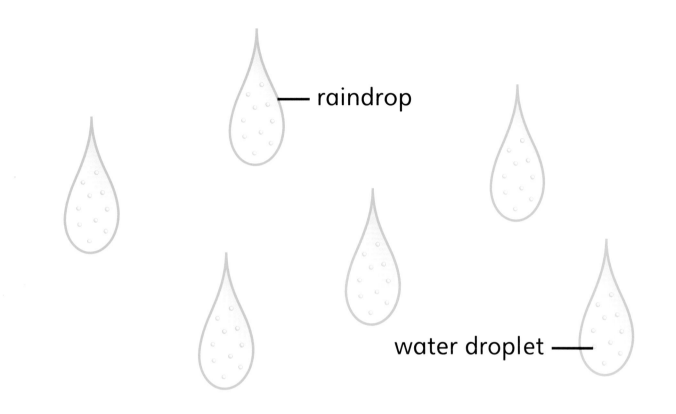

raindrop

water droplet ——

A raindrop is made from tiny drops of water. Each tiny drop is called a water droplet.

water droplet —

water vapour —

When the sun warms water,
some of the water becomes
water vapour.

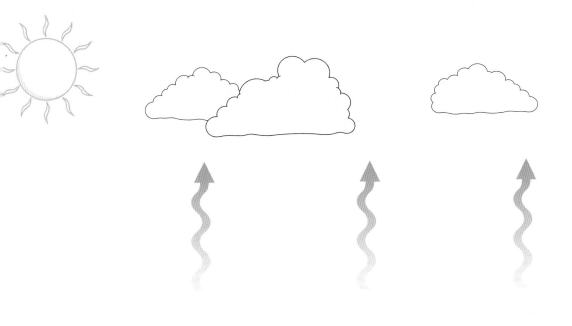

Water vapour is air that is full of moisture.

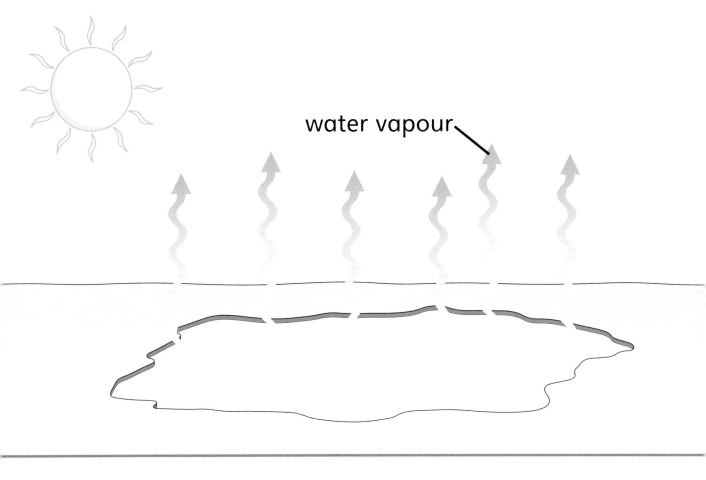

water vapour

Water vapour comes
from oceans and lakes.

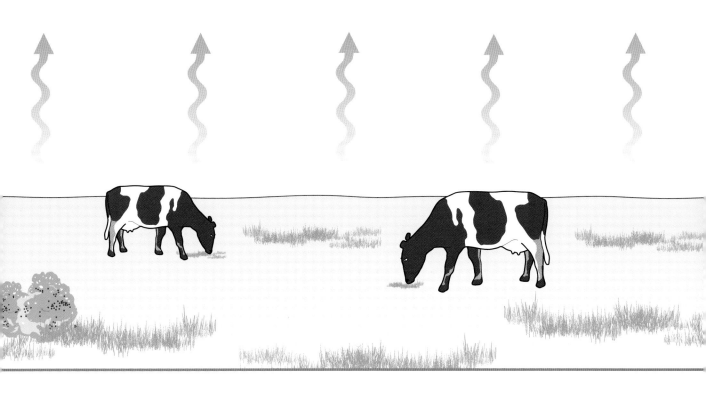

Water vapour comes
from plants and animals.

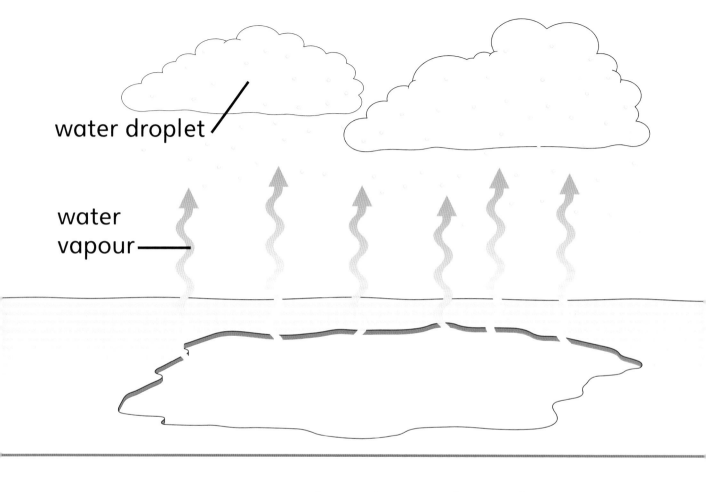

water droplet

water vapour

Water vapour rises into the air.
As it cools, it forms water droplets.
These water droplets make clouds.

raindrop

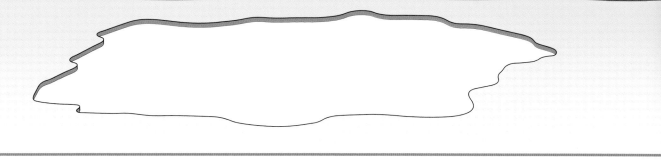

In the clouds, the droplets join
together and form raindrops.
The raindrops fall down to earth.

13

Types of rain

Sometimes the rain is light.

Sometimes the rain is heavy.

Sometimes it does not rain for a long time. There is not enough water.

This is called a drought.

Sometimes it rains too much.
There is too much water.

This is called a flood.

How does rain help us?

All living things need water.
Rain brings water back to the earth.

A rainy day can be fun!

What to wear in the rain

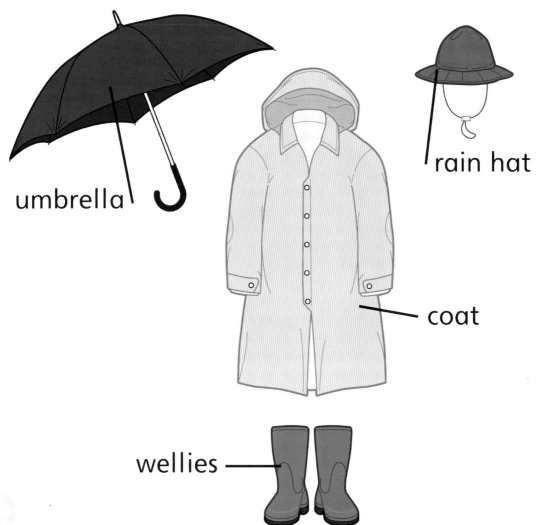

umbrella

rain hat

coat

wellies

Picture glossary

 **drought** when it does not rain for a long time

 **flood** when there is too much water on the land

 **water droplet** a tiny drop of water. Water droplets are smaller than raindrops.

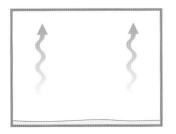 **water vapour** air that is full of moisture

Index

cloud 6, 12, 13
drought 17
flood 19
raindrop 7, 13

water droplet 7, 8, 12, 13
water vapour 8, 9, 10, 11, 12

Notes to parents and teachers

Before reading

Talk about different weather. Ask the children which type of weather they like best. Have they ever been out in the rain? What did it feel like?

After reading

Try the Water Cycle experiment: Place a tumbler in the centre of a glass mixing bowl. Pour boiling water around the tumbler. Cover the bowl with cling film. Place a pebble over the top of the glass. As the water evaporates talk about the water cooling and condensing on the cling film and falling like raindrops into the tumbler. Draw a simple diagram of the water cycle. Ask the children to help you to label the raindrops, the water droplets, the cloud, and the water vapour.

Titles in the *Weather Watchers* series include:

Hardback 0 431 18258 2

Hardback 0 431 18256 6

Hardback 0 431 18257 4

Hardback 0 431 18259 0

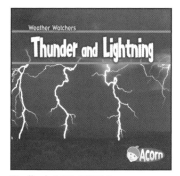

Hardback 0 431 18255 8

Hardback 0 431 18260 4

Find out about other titles from Heinemann Library on our website www.heinemann.co.uk/library